Miracles of Artificial Intelligence In Daily Life

(Exploring the Wonders of AI)

By

Kashaf

TABLE OF CONTENT

Chapter 1

Introduction to AI

Artificial Intelligence (AI) stands at the forefront of technological innovation, promising to revolutionize the way we live, work, and interact with the world around us. At its core, AI refers to the simulation of human intelligence in machines, enabling them to perform tasks that typically require human cognition, such as learning, problem-solving, and decision-making. The journey of AI began several decades ago, rooted in the desire to create machines that could mimic human intelligence. Early pioneers laid the groundwork for AI development, with breakthroughs in areas such as symbolic reasoning, neural networks, and machine learning paving the way for the modern AI landscape we see today.

The concept of AI encompasses a spectrum of capabilities, ranging from narrow AI, which is designed for specific tasks, to the hypothetical notion of general AI, which would possess human-level intelligence across a wide range of domains. Narrow AI systems, also known as weak AI, are prevalent in our daily lives, powering applications such as virtual assistants, recommendation algorithms, and autonomous vehicles. These systems excel at performing well-defined tasks within constrained environments, leveraging techniques such as supervised learning, reinforcement learning, and natural language processing to achieve their objectives.

The proliferation of AI has been fueled by exponential advancements in computing power, data availability, and algorithmic sophistication. In recent years, the rise of big data and cloud computing has provided AI researchers and practitioners with access to vast amounts of information and computational resources, enabling them to train increasingly complex models and tackle previously insurmountable challenges. Additionally, breakthroughs in deep learning, a subfield of machine learning inspired by the structure and function of the human brain, have propelled AI performance to unprecedented levels, leading to remarkable achievements in areas such as image recognition, speech recognition, and natural language understanding.

The impact of AI on society is profound and multifaceted, touching nearly every aspect of human existence. From healthcare to finance, transportation to entertainment, AI is reshaping industries and redefining the way we live our lives. In healthcare, AI-driven technologies are revolutionizing medical diagnosis and treatment, enabling early detection of diseases, personalized treatment plans, and improved patient outcomes. In education, AI-powered learning platforms are providing students with personalized learning experiences tailored to their individual needs and learning styles, while also empowering educators with valuable insights into student progress and performance.

Despite its transformative potential, AI is not without its challenges and controversies. Ethical considerations, such as algorithmic bias, privacy concerns, and job displacement, loom large in discussions surrounding AI adoption and regulation. The opaque nature of some AI systems, particularly those based on deep learning algorithms, raises questions about accountability, transparency, and the potential for unintended consequences. Moreover, the unequal distribution of AI benefits and risks across different segments of society exacerbates existing disparities and underscores the importance of equitable AI development and deployment.

Looking ahead, the future of AI holds both promise and peril. As AI continues to evolve and permeate all aspects of human society, it is essential to approach its development and deployment with caution and foresight. Ethical considerations must be front and center in AI research and practice, guiding decisions about algorithm design, data collection, and system deployment. Moreover, collaboration and dialogue among stakeholders from diverse backgrounds and perspectives are crucial for addressing the complex societal challenges posed by AI and ensuring that its benefits are shared equitably among all members of society. Ultimately, the miracles of AI in daily life are not predetermined; rather, they depend on the choices we make today and the actions we take tomorrow to harness the transformative power of AI for the greater good.

Chapter 2

AI in Healthcare

In the realm of healthcare, the integration of Artificial Intelligence (AI) represents a paradigm shift, promising to revolutionize medical diagnosis, treatment, and patient care. The application of AI in healthcare is multifaceted, encompassing a wide range of tasks, from medical imaging analysis to drug discovery, clinical decision support, and personalized medicine. One of the most significant contributions of AI to healthcare lies in its ability to analyze complex medical data with speed and precision, enabling clinicians to make more accurate diagnoses and develop tailored treatment plans for patients.

Medical imaging is a prime example of how AI is transforming healthcare. AI-powered image analysis systems can interpret medical images, such as Xrays, MRIs, and CT scans, with a level of accuracy that rivals or even surpasses human radiologists. These systems can detect subtle abnormalities, such as tumors or fractures, that might be overlooked by human eyes, leading to earlier detection and treatment of diseases. Moreover, AI algorithms can analyze large volumes of imaging data to identify patterns and trends that may not be apparent to human observers, thereby facilitating research into disease mechanisms and treatment outcomes.

Another area where AI is making a significant impact in healthcare is in the realm of predictive analytics and clinical decision support. By analyzing electronic health records (EHRs), genomic data, and other relevant information, AI algorithms can identify patients at high risk for certain diseases or complications, allowing healthcare providers to intervene proactively and prevent adverse outcomes. Additionally, AI-based decision support systems can assist clinicians in making informed treatment decisions by synthesizing vast amounts of medical literature, patient data, and clinical guidelines to recommend the most appropriate course of action for individual patients.

Personalized medicine, which aims to tailor medical treatment to the unique characteristics of each patient, is another area where AI holds great promise. By analyzing genomic data, biomarkers, and other patient-specific information, AI algorithms can identify optimal treatment regimens that are tailored to the individual's genetic makeup, disease profile, and lifestyle factors. This personalized approach to medicine has the potential to improve treatment efficacy, reduce adverse drug reactions, and enhance patient outcomes, ushering in a new era of precision medicine.

In addition to improving diagnostic accuracy and treatment efficacy, AI is also transforming the way healthcare is delivered to patients. Virtual health assistants, powered by AI technologies such as natural language processing and machine learning, are enabling patients to access healthcare services and information remotely, anytime and anywhere. These virtual assistants can answer medical questions, schedule appointments, refill prescriptions, and provide personalized health recommendations, thereby increasing access to care and empowering patients to take control of their health.

Despite its tremendous potential, the widespread adoption of AI in healthcare is not without challenges. Ethical considerations, such as patient privacy, data security, and algorithmic bias, must be carefully addressed to ensure that AI technologies are deployed in a responsible and equitable manner. Moreover, the integration of AI into clinical workflows requires collaboration and coordination among healthcare providers, technology developers, regulatory agencies, and other stakeholders to overcome barriers such as interoperability, usability, and regulatory compliance.

Looking ahead, the future of AI in healthcare holds great promise for improving patient outcomes, enhancing clinical decision-making, and transforming the delivery of healthcare services. By harnessing the power of AI to analyze vast amounts of medical data, identify actionable insights, and personalize treatment approaches, we have the opportunity to revolutionize healthcare and usher in a new era of precision medicine.

However, realizing this vision will require continued investment in research and development, collaboration across disciplines, and a commitment to addressing the ethical, regulatory, and practical challenges that accompany the integration of AI into healthcare.

Chapter 3

AI in Education

The intersection of Artificial Intelligence (AI) and education holds immense potential to transform learning and teaching practices, ushering in a new era of personalized, adaptive, and data-driven education. AI technologies are increasingly being integrated into educational settings, offering innovative solutions to age-old challenges such as student engagement, personalized learning, and educational equity. From intelligent tutoring systems to adaptive learning platforms and automated grading tools, AI is reshaping the landscape of education, promising to enhance learning outcomes and empower both students and educators.

One of the primary applications of AI in education is personalized learning, which tailors instruction to the individual needs, preferences, and learning styles of each student. AI-powered adaptive learning platforms analyze student performance data in real-time, identifying areas of strength and weakness, and dynamically adjusting the content and pace of instruction to optimize learning outcomes. By providing personalized learning experiences that are tailored to the unique needs of each learner, these platforms can improve student engagement, motivation, and retention, fostering deeper conceptual understanding and mastery of academic concepts.

Intelligent tutoring systems represent another promising application of AI in education. These systems leverage AI algorithms to provide individualized instruction and support to students, offering immediate feedback, scaffolding, and guidance as they work through learning activities and assignments. By simulating one-on-one tutoring interactions with virtual tutors, intelligent tutoring systems can enhance student learning outcomes, improve problem-solving skills, and promote metacognitive awareness. Moreover, these systems can adapt to the student's level of proficiency and learning trajectory, providing targeted interventions and remediation as needed to address areas of difficulty.

AI technologies are also revolutionizing assessment and evaluation practices in education. Automated grading tools powered by AI algorithms can analyze student responses to quizzes, assignments, and exams, providing instant feedback and assessment of student performance. These tools not only save time for educators but also enable more frequent and formative assessment practices, allowing students to receive timely feedback on their progress and identify areas for improvement. Additionally, AI-driven assessment tools can generate actionable insights into student learning patterns and misconceptions, informing instructional decision-making and curriculum design.

Another area where AI is making a significant impact in education is in the realm of educational content creation and curation. AI algorithms can analyze vast amounts of educational resources, such as textbooks, articles, videos, and simulations, to identify relevant and high-quality materials that align with curriculum standards and learning objectives. These content curation tools can help educators save time and effort in searching for and selecting instructional materials, ensuring that students have access to diverse, engaging, and pedagogically sound resources to support their learning.

Despite its potential benefits, the widespread adoption of AI in education is not without challenges and limitations. Ethical considerations, such as data privacy, algorithmic bias, and equity in access to AI-driven educational technologies, must be carefully addressed to ensure that AI enhances, rather than exacerbates, existing disparities in educational opportunities and outcomes. Moreover, the integration of AI into educational settings requires thoughtful planning, professional development, and support to empower educators to effectively leverage AI technologies in their teaching practice.

Looking ahead, the future of AI in education holds great promise for improving learning outcomes, enhancing instructional effectiveness, and fostering educational equity. By harnessing the power of AI to personalize learning experiences, provide intelligent tutoring and assessment, and curate educational content, we have the opportunity to create more engaging, effective, and inclusive learning environments for all students. However, realizing this vision will require collaboration and partnership among educators, researchers, policymakers, and technology developers to overcome challenges, address ethical concerns, and ensure that AI is used responsibly and ethically to support the diverse needs of learners around the world.

Chapter 4

AI in Transportation

The integration of Artificial Intelligence (AI) into transportation systems is poised to revolutionize the way people and goods move from one place to another. From autonomous vehicles to traffic management systems and predictive maintenance, AI is driving innovation and efficiency in transportation, offering solutions to longstanding challenges such as traffic congestion, road safety, and environmental sustainability. By harnessing the power of AI to analyze data, optimize operations, and enhance decision-making, transportation stakeholders have the opportunity to create safer, more reliable, and sustainable transportation networks for the future.

Autonomous vehicles represent one of the most visible applications of AI in transportation. These self-driving cars, trucks, and drones leverage AI algorithms, sensors, and actuators to perceive their environment, navigate roads, and make real-time driving decisions without human intervention. By eliminating the need for human drivers, autonomous vehicles have the potential to improve road safety, reduce traffic congestion, and increase mobility for individuals who are unable to drive. Moreover, autonomous vehicle technology holds promise for revolutionizing the logistics and transportation industries, enabling more efficient and cost-effective movement of goods and services.

In addition to autonomous vehicles, AI is also being used to optimize traffic flow and reduce congestion in urban areas. Traffic management systems powered by AI algorithms can analyze real-time traffic data from sensors, cameras, and other sources to predict traffic patterns, identify bottlenecks, and dynamically adjust signal timing and lane configurations to improve traffic flow. By coordinating traffic signals, managing lane usage, and prioritizing public transportation, these systems can reduce travel times, minimize delays, and enhance overall transportation efficiency in urban areas.

Predictive maintenance is another area where AI is making a significant impact in transportation. By analyzing data from sensors, IoT devices, and maintenance records, AI algorithms can predict when critical transportation infrastructure, such as roads, bridges, and transit systems, is likely to fail or require maintenance. This proactive approach to maintenance allows transportation agencies to prioritize repairs, allocate resources more effectively, and minimize disruptions to travel and commerce. Moreover, predictive maintenance can help extend the lifespan of transportation assets, reduce maintenance costs, and improve overall system reliability and resilience.

AI technologies are also being used to enhance the efficiency and sustainability of public transportation systems. Intelligent transit systems powered by AI algorithms can optimize route planning, scheduling, and fleet management to maximize service reliability, minimize wait times, and reduce energy consumption. Additionally, AI-driven predictive analytics can help transit agencies anticipate demand patterns, adjust service levels in real-time, and provide personalized travel information to passengers, enhancing the overall passenger experience and encouraging greater adoption of public transportation.

Despite its potential benefits, the widespread adoption of AI in transportation is not without challenges and concerns. Ethical considerations, such as safety, privacy, and liability, must be carefully addressed to ensure the safe and responsible deployment of AI-driven transportation technologies. Moreover, the integration of AI into transportation systems requires collaboration and coordination among government agencies, industry stakeholders, and the public to address regulatory, technical, and societal barriers to adoption.

Looking ahead, the future of AI in transportation holds great promise for improving mobility, safety, and sustainability in cities and communities around the world. By harnessing the power of AI to optimize traffic flow, enable autonomous vehicles, and enhance public transportation systems, we have the opportunity to create more efficient, equitable, and resilient transportation networks that meet the needs of people and businesses in the 21st century. However, realizing this vision will require continued investment in research and development, collaboration among stakeholders, and a commitment to addressing the complex challenges and opportunities that lie ahead in the intersection of AI and transportation.

Chapter 5

AI in Finance

The integration of Artificial Intelligence (AI) into the financial sector is reshaping the way financial institutions operate, make decisions, and interact with customers. From algorithmic trading to fraud detection and personalized financial advice, AI is driving innovation and efficiency in finance, offering solutions to longstanding challenges such as risk management, customer service, and regulatory compliance. By leveraging the power of AI to analyze data, automate processes, and optimize decision-making, financial institutions have the opportunity to enhance their competitiveness, improve customer experience, and mitigate risks in an increasingly complex and dynamic global marketplace.

Algorithmic trading represents one of the most prominent applications of AI in finance. These automated trading systems use AI algorithms to analyze market data, identify trading opportunities, and execute trades at speeds and frequencies that are beyond the capabilities of human traders. By leveraging machine learning and natural language processing techniques, algorithmic trading systems can interpret market signals, news events, and social media sentiment to make informed trading decisions, leading to improved trading performance and liquidity in financial markets.

Fraud detection and prevention is another area where AI is making a significant impact in finance. AI-powered fraud detection systems analyze transaction data, user behavior, and other relevant information to identify suspicious patterns and anomalies that may indicate fraudulent activity. By leveraging advanced analytics and machine learning algorithms, these systems can detect fraud in real-time, enabling financial institutions to take immediate action to mitigate losses and protect customers' assets and identities. Moreover, AI-driven fraud detection systems can adapt and evolve over time to detect new and emerging fraud schemes, staying one step ahead of cybercriminals.

Risk management is a critical function in the financial industry, and AI technologies are increasingly being used to assess, monitor, and mitigate risks across various dimensions, such as credit risk, market risk, and operational risk. AI-powered risk management systems can analyze vast amounts of data, including financial statements, market data, and macroeconomic indicators, to identify potential risks and vulnerabilities in financial portfolios and transactions. By providing real-time insights and predictive analytics, these systems enable financial institutions to make informed risk management decisions and protect against unforeseen events and market fluctuations.

Personalized financial advice and wealth management is another area where AI is transforming the financial services industry. AI-powered robo-advisors use algorithms to analyze investors' financial goals, risk tolerance, and investment preferences to create personalized investment portfolios and provide ongoing portfolio management and rebalancing services. By automating the investment process and offering low-cost, accessible investment solutions, robo-advisors democratize wealth management and empower individuals to achieve their financial goals without the need for traditional human advisors.

Despite its potential benefits, the widespread adoption of AI in finance is not without challenges and concerns. Ethical considerations, such as data privacy, algorithmic bias, and transparency, must be carefully addressed to ensure that AI-driven financial technologies are deployed in a responsible and ethical manner. Moreover, the integration of AI into financial systems requires robust cybersecurity measures and regulatory oversight to protect against potential risks and vulnerabilities, such as cyber attacks, data breaches, and market manipulation.

Looking ahead, the future of AI in finance holds great promise for improving financial inclusion, increasing efficiency, and reducing risks in the global financial system. By harnessing the power of AI to automate processes, enhance decision-making, and personalize services, financial institutions can create more resilient, responsive, and customer-centric financial services that meet the evolving needs of consumers and businesses in the digital age. However, realizing this vision will require collaboration among industry stakeholders, policymakers, and regulators to address challenges, build trust, and ensure that AI is used responsibly and ethically to promote financial stability and well-being.

Chapter 6

AI in Entertainment and Media

The entertainment and media industries are undergoing a profound transformation fueled by advances in Artificial Intelligence (AI) technologies. From content creation to distribution and audience engagement, AI is revolutionizing how we produce, consume, and interact with media content. This chapter explores the myriad ways in which AI is reshaping the entertainment landscape, from generating music and movies to personalizing content recommendations and creating virtual influencers.

One of the most significant applications of AI in entertainment is in content creation. AI algorithms can analyze vast amounts of data, including images, videos, and text, to generate original content such as music, art, and even literature. For example, AI-powered music composition tools can generate original melodies, harmonies, and arrangements based on input from composers or musical styles, enabling artists to explore new creative possibilities and accelerate the music production process. Similarly, AI-driven tools can generate artwork and visual effects for films, animations, and video games, reducing production costs and enhancing the visual appeal of multimedia content.

In addition to content creation, AI is also transforming the way content is distributed and consumed. Recommendation systems powered by AI algorithms analyze user preferences, behavior, and interactions to personalize content recommendations across various platforms, such as streaming services, social media, and e-commerce sites.

These recommendation engines use techniques such as collaborative filtering, content-based filtering, and deep learning to identify relevant content that matches users' interests and preferences, thereby enhancing user engagement and satisfaction.

Virtual influencers are another emerging trend in the entertainment industry, driven by advancements in AI and digital media technologies. These computer-generated characters, often indistinguishable from real humans, have amassed large followings on social media platforms such as Instagram and TikTok, where they promote brands, products, and lifestyles to their virtual audiences. By leveraging AI algorithms to generate lifelike animations, voice synthesis, and personality traits, virtual influencers offer advertisers a novel way to connect with consumers and drive engagement without the need for human influencers.

AI technologies are also being used to enhance the storytelling and interactive experiences in video games and immersive media. AI-powered game engines can dynamically generate game worlds, characters, and narratives based on player interactions, enabling more immersive and personalized gaming experiences. Additionally, AI-driven chatbots and virtual assistants can enhance player engagement and immersion by providing interactive dialogue, guidance, and feedback within games and virtual environments.

Despite its transformative potential, the integration of AI into entertainment and media is not without challenges and controversies. Ethical considerations, such as algorithmic bias, privacy concerns, and the potential for manipulation and misinformation, must be carefully addressed to ensure that AI-driven content creation and distribution are used responsibly and ethically. Moreover, the rise of AI-generated content raises questions about copyright, ownership, and authorship in the digital age, prompting policymakers, industry stakeholders, and content creators to grapple with issues of intellectual property and creative attribution.

Looking ahead, the future of AI in entertainment and media holds great promise for expanding creative possibilities, enhancing user experiences, and democratizing access to content creation and distribution. By harnessing the power of AI to generate original content, personalize recommendations, and create immersive interactive experiences, the entertainment industry can unlock new opportunities for innovation and engagement in a rapidly evolving digital landscape. However, realizing this vision will require collaboration among content creators, technologists, regulators, and consumers to address ethical concerns, ensure transparency and accountability, and foster a vibrant and inclusive ecosystem for AI-driven entertainment and media.

Chapter 7

The Future of AI

The future of Artificial Intelligence (AI) holds both promise and uncertainty as the technology continues to evolve and permeate every aspect of human society. This chapter explores the potential directions of AI development and its implications for humanity, highlighting the opportunities and challenges that lie ahead in harnessing the full potential of AI for the benefit of society.

One of the key areas of focus for the future of AI is human-AI collaboration. As AI technologies become more advanced and capable, there is increasing interest in exploring how humans and machines can work together synergistically to solve complex problems and achieve shared goals. Human-AI collaboration holds the potential to augment human capabilities, enhance productivity, and drive innovation across various domains, from healthcare and education to finance and manufacturing.

Explainable AI (XAI) is another important area of research and development in AI. As AI systems become more complex and opaque, there is a growing need to develop methods and techniques that enable humans to understand and interpret the decisions and behaviors of AI systems. XAI seeks to make AI systems more transparent, accountable, and trustworthy by providing insights into the underlying algorithms, data, and reasoning processes that drive their behavior.

Ethical AI development and deployment is a critical consideration for the future of AI. As AI technologies become more integrated into society, there are concerns about the potential for algorithmic bias, discrimination, and unintended consequences. It is essential to ensure that AI systems are developed and deployed in a manner that upholds ethical principles, respects human rights, and promotes fairness, accountability, and transparency.

The democratization of AI is another key trend shaping the future of the technology. As AI becomes more accessible and affordable, there is a growing democratization of access to AI tools, resources, and expertise. This democratization has the potential to empower individuals and communities to harness the power of AI for social good, innovation, and economic development.

The future of AI also raises questions about the impact of automation on the workforce and society. While AI has the potential to enhance productivity, efficiency, and economic growth, it also poses challenges related to job displacement, income inequality, and the future of work. It is essential to explore strategies for managing the transition to an AI-driven economy, including reskilling and upskilling workers, fostering entrepreneurship, and ensuring social safety nets for those affected by automation.

Looking ahead, the future of AI holds tremendous promise for addressing some of the most pressing challenges facing humanity, from climate change and healthcare to education and social justice. By harnessing the power of AI to analyze complex data, solve complex problems, and augment human intelligence, we have the opportunity to unlock new frontiers of knowledge, innovation, and human potential.

However, realizing this vision will require collaboration and cooperation among governments, industry stakeholders, researchers, and civil society organizations to address the ethical, social, and economic implications of AI. It is essential to foster an inclusive and participatory dialogue about the future of AI that engages diverse perspectives and stakeholders, promotes transparency and accountability, and ensures that AI technologies are developed and deployed in a manner that promotes the well-being and prosperity of all members of society.

_____THE END_____

www.ingramcontent.com/pod-product-compliance
Lightning Source LLC
LaVergne TN
LVHW051627050326
832903LV00033B/4703